LITTLE KIDS
FIRST
BIG
BOOK OF THE
RAIN FOREST

Moira Rose Donohue

NATIONAL GEOGRAPHIC KiDS

WASHINGTON, D.C.

CONTENTS

INTRODUCTION

This book introduces Earth's rain forests and explores them through the animals that live there. It answers questions from "What is a rain forest?" and "How much does it rain in a rain forest?" to "Why are poison dart frogs poisonous?" Although some rain forests grow in cooler parts of the world, most are found in the tropics, where it is warm all year. The animals featured in this book all live in tropical rain forests. A map at the back of the book shows where each of these animals is found in the wild.

CHAPTER ONE begins the book with a look at what makes a rain forest a rain forest. It introduces young readers to the four levels of this ecosystem: the forest floor, understory, canopy, and emergent layer. This chapter also highlights some of the amazing plants that grow in rain forests.

CHAPTER TWO continues the exploration of rain forests with a visit to the bottom level: the forest floor. Here readers will meet snakes, spiders, frogs, mandrills, and other animals that slither, creep, hop, or walk on or near the ground.

CHAPTER THREE examines the second level of the rain forest: the understory.

Gigantic beetles, long-tongued lizards, and sleek jaguars are some of the animals observed in this chapter.

CHAPTER FOUR covers the third level, the canopy, which contains the branches and leaves of the giant trees that stretch across the rain forest. Slow-moving sloths, leaping lemurs, and big-beaked birds are among the animals featured here.

CHAPTER FIVE wraps up the main sections of the book with a trip to the highest level of the rain forest, the emergent layer. Enormous eagles and rainbow-colored butterflies are some of the creatures that swoop and flutter through the tip-top of the tallest trees.

HOW TO USE THIS BOOK

Colorful **PHOTOGRAPHS** illustrate each spread and support the text.

POP-UP FACTS throughout provide added information about the rain forest and the animals featured in each section.

ROUGH SCALES help protect the eyelash viper's body from **SPIKY** tree **BRANCHES.**

UNDERSTORY

EYELASH VIPER
This beautiful snake has a deadly bite.

The eyelash viper can be yellow, green, brown, or even light blue. Its head is shaped like a triangle. This snake looks like it has eyelashes. But those are actually pointy scales.

The eyelash viper **BITES ITS PREY** with venom-filled **FANGS** to kill it.

The viper loops itself around trees, vines, flowers, and fruits in the understory. Its color helps it blend in with a plant or flower while it waits for its prey to come close. Hummingbirds are a favorite meal.

Feel your eyelashes—are they soft or scaly?

FACTS

KIND OF ANIMAL
reptile

HOME
Central and northern South America

SIZE
nearly as long as a guitar

FOOD
frogs, lizards, small birds, and mice

SOUNDS
soft slurping

BABIES
six to 20 live babies at a time

62

63

FACT BOXES give the young reader a quick look at an animal's basic biology: the kind of animal it is, where it lives, how big it is, what it eats, the sounds it makes, and how many young it has at a time.

INTERACTIVE QUESTIONS in each section encourage conversation related to the topic.

MORE FOR PARENTS in the back of the book offers parent tips that include fun activities that relate to rain forests, and a helpful glossary.

CHAPTER 1
RAIN FOREST BASICS

Welcome to the rain forest. You might want your umbrella. In this chapter, you will learn why.

RAINDROPS KEEP FALLING

It rains nearly **EVERY DAY** in a **RAIN FOREST.**

Drip, drip, pitter, patter. Here comes the rain!
Rain forests are woodlands that get lots and lots of rain. They are filled with leafy plants and trees growing very close together. Rain forests are also home to countless numbers of animals.

Some rain forests grow in cooler parts of the world, along coasts. They are called temperate rain forests.

Most rain forests are found in the tropics, the parts of Earth near the Equator, where it stays warm all year. They are called tropical rain forests, or jungles. All the animals in this book live in tropical rain forests.

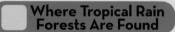

The **AMAZON RAIN FOREST** in South America is the **LARGEST** rain forest on **EARTH.** It is a **TROPICAL FOREST.**

Where Tropical Rain Forests Are Found

NORTH AMERICA

EUROPE

ASIA

ATLANTIC OCEAN

AFRICA

PACIFIC OCEAN

EQUATOR

INDIAN OCEAN

PACIFIC OCEAN

SOUTH AMERICA

AUSTRALIA

ANTARCTICA

11

RAIN FOREST LAYERS

The **TOP LAYER** is called the **EMERGENT LAYER**. It is made up of the **VERY TALLEST TREETOPS**, which poke above the canopy layer.

The **THIRD LAYER** is the **CANOPY**. It contains the **LEAVES** and **BRANCHES** of the tall trees that stretch over the rain forest like giant green umbrellas.

A rain forest can be divided into four levels, or layers. Each layer is like a different neighborhood, with different kinds of animals living there. Some animals spend their entire life in one layer. Others move between the layers to find food.

EMERGENT LAYER

CANOPY

UNDERSTORY

FOREST FLOOR

The **SECOND LAYER** is the **UNDERSTORY**. It is filled with **SMALL TREES** and **TANGLED VINES.**

The **BOTTOM LAYER** is the **FOREST FLOOR.** It is covered with **ROOTS** and **ROTTING LEAVES.** It is dark and shady, because the trees above it block most of the light. Rivers flow through some parts of the forest floor.

BROMELIADS

WONDERFUL PLANTS

Tall trees, short trees, trees with big leaves, trees with small leaves. There are many different kinds of trees in rain forests.

Mosses, ferns, and beautiful flowers called orchids grow on the bark of many trees. Cup-shaped plants called bromeliads grow there too. They fill with water when it rains. Many creatures drink water from these pools.

ORCHIDS

RAFFLESIA

Rain forests are also filled with vines. Thick, woody vines called lianas twist up tree trunks and loop through branches.

The **RAFFLESIA** plant has the **WORLD'S LARGEST FLOWER.** It's bigger than a car tire! This plant **GROWS** in rain forests in Southeast Asia.

LIANA

15

CHAPTER 2
ROAMING THE FOREST FLOOR

In this chapter you will meet the creatures that live in the bottom layer of the rain forest.

FACTS

KIND OF ANIMAL
mammal

HOME
western central Africa

SIZE
half as tall as a grown man

FOOD
fruits, roots, insects, and reptiles

SOUNDS
screams, roars, and grunts

BABIES
one at a time

MALE

A mandrill has a **POUCH** inside its **CHEEK** that it uses to store food to **SNACK** on later.

What foods do you like to snack on?

MANDRILL

This colorful creature is a kind of monkey.

Male mandrills look as if they had their faces painted at the fair. They have brighter colors than the females.

A mandrill walks on all fours. It uses its long arms to search the ground for fruits, roots, and small animals to eat.

Though mandrills spend most of their time on the forest floor, they climb into trees to sleep. Sometimes they look for food in the trees.

FEMALE

BABY

CAPYBARA

The capybara lives near ponds and rivers.

SAY MY NAME: kah-pee-BAR-uh

It can **HOLD ITS BREATH** underwater for up to **FIVE MINUTES.**

Capybaras look kind of like hairy pigs without a snout. But they are not pigs. Capybaras are related to rats, squirrels, and hamsters. They have long front teeth that never stop growing.

The capybara uses its **WEBBED FEET** to **SWIM** and to **WALK.**

FACTS

KIND OF ANIMAL
mammal

HOME
South America

SIZE
about the size of a
large dog

FOOD
grass and water plants,
and sometimes melons

SOUNDS
soft whinnies, squeals,
and chitters

BABIES
up to eight at a time

How do you cool off when it's hot?

To stay cool during the heat of day, a
capybara spends much of its time in the
water. It also hides in the water from
animals that want to eat it, such as jaguars.

GREEN ANACONDA
This snake has a big mouth.

An anaconda can go **WEEKS** or **MONTHS WITHOUT FOOD** after a big meal.

This snake's green-and-brown skin helps hide it in muddy water. It floats just under the surface of the water while it waits for prey.

A **GROUP** of anacondas is **CALLED** a bed or a **KNOT.**

The anaconda is not a poisonous snake. It is a constrictor. A constrictor grabs its prey with its mouth. Then the snake coils its body around the animal and squeezes it to kill it.

The green anaconda can **WEIGH** up to **550 POUNDS** (250 kg). That's about as much as **14** five-year-old **KIDS!**

The anaconda opens its jaws wide and swallows its meal whole. Really big green anacondas can gulp down a jaguar or wild pig!

FACTS

KIND OF ANIMAL
reptile

HOME
northern South America

SIZE
about as long as a pickup truck

FOOD
fish, birds, wild pigs, and other mammals

SOUNDS
hoarse bark or hiss

BABIES
20 to 40 live babies at a time

How wide can you open your mouth?

BLUE POISON DART FROG

This little frog gleams like a gem on the rain forest floor.

Scientists think poison dart frogs may be **POISONOUS** because of **SOME INSECTS** they **EAT.**

24

The blue poison dart frog's bright color warns predators: *Don't eat me or you might get sick!* The frog's skin oozes a strong poison that can kill other animals.

Female blue poison dart frogs lay eggs on the forest floor. When the eggs hatch into tadpoles, the mother and father frog carry them on their backs to small pools of water, often in bromeliad plants.

This poison dart frog **TADPOLE** has **SPROUTED LEGS** but still has a **TAIL.**

FACTS

KIND OF ANIMAL
amphibian

HOME
South America

SIZE
as long as a child's finger

FOOD
termites, ants, and other small insects

SOUNDS
chirps and buzzes

BABIES
two to six eggs at a time

As the tadpoles grow, their bodies change. They sprout legs. Their tails get smaller and smaller. After several months, they look like frogs and climb out of the pool.

Can you think of another animal that is brightly colored?

GOLDEN POISON DART FROG

There are more than 100 kinds of **POISON DART FROGS** in Central and South American rain forests. Here are a few.

HARLEQUIN POISON DART FROG

GREEN AND BLACK POISON DART FROG

RETICULATED POISON DART FROG

STRAWBERRY POISON DART FROG

YELLOW-BANDED POISON DART FROG

AMAZON RIVER DOLPHIN

The Amazon river dolphin is also called the pink dolphin.

These dolphins sometimes **SWIM UPSIDE DOWN.**

Most kinds of dolphins live in the ocean, in salt water. But this dolphin is found in the freshwater river that winds through the Amazon rain forest.

Some Amazon river dolphins are bluish gray. Many others are pink, and they can get even pinker when they are excited.

FOREST FLOOR

FACTS

KIND OF ANIMAL
mammal

HOME
South America

SIZE
about as long as a bed

FOOD
fish, shrimp, and crabs

SOUNDS
buzzes and clicks

BABIES
one at a time

Like all **DOLPHINS,** Amazon river dolphins are **MAMMALS.** They must come to the surface to **BREATHE AIR.**

Amazon river dolphins use their long, skinny snouts to nudge crabs and other food up from the river bottom.

Can you name three things that are pink?

29

Its long **SNOUT** helps this animal **DIG** for **FOOD** on the forest floor.

FACTS

KIND OF ANIMAL
mammal

HOME
Madagascar, Africa

SIZE
about as long as a coloring marker

FOOD
worms

SOUNDS
chirps, crunches, and *putt-putt* sounds

BABIES
two to 11 at a time

Can you think of another animal with black and yellow stripes? Hint: It buzzes.

LOWLAND STREAKED TENREC

This little animal is covered with sharp quills.

When a predator is near, the sharp golden quills around the tenrec's neck stand straight up. That's a warning: Move on! Predators that don't take the hint might get stabbed. Sometimes this spiny creature shakes a few quills loose, and they get stuck in its attacker.

The lowland streaked tenrec has a few special quills. It rubs them together to make sounds that other tenrecs can hear.

The lowland streaked tenrec has **BLACK** and **YELLOW STRIPES** down its back.

LOWLAND TAPIR

This animal has an extra-long nose.

The lowland tapir has black or brownish gray bristly fur and a short ridge, or mane, of hair on its head and shoulders.

This animal's long snout, or trunk, helps it smell a predator nearby. The tapir also uses its snout to pluck leaves and fruit off trees.

What other animal has a trunk that it uses to feed itself?

FACTS

KIND OF ANIMAL
mammal

HOME
South America

SIZE
about as tall as a
five-year-old child

FOOD
fruits and leaves

SOUNDS
shrieks, clicks,
and snorts

BABIES
one at a time

BABY

ADULT

SPOTS and **STRIPES** on a **BABY TAPIR** help hide it from hungry animals. The **MARKINGS** blend in with leaves and **SHADOWS.**

33

SOUTHERN CASSOWARY

This big bird with tiny wings cannot fly.

SAY MY NAME: KASS-uh-ware-ee

The southern cassowary is the second heaviest bird in the world. Only the ostrich weighs more. Like ostriches, southern cassowaries cannot fly.

FACTS

KIND OF ANIMAL
bird

HOME
Australia, New Guinea

SIZE
when it stretches up, about as tall as an average-size female human

FOOD
berries, other fruits, and leaves

SOUNDS
rumbles, hisses, and low bellows

BABIES
three to seven eggs

CASQUE

This bird's **CASQUE** is covered with the same material that makes up **HUMAN FINGERNAILS.**

CHICK

The cassowary has a long, colorful neck. Its head is topped with a tall, hornlike bump called a casque (CASK).

A cassowary has three toes on each foot. Its inside toe has a long, sharp claw, which it uses for scratching or fighting.

SHARP CLAW

EGGS

A mother cassowary lays green eggs. Then the male sits on the eggs. After they hatch, the father bird looks after the chicks for nine months or longer.

Southern cassowaries eat a lot of berries and other fruits. As the birds wander, they carry the seeds of the fruits in their bodies. When the birds poop, the seeds land in different parts of the rain forest. Some of the seeds will sprout and grow into new plants.

LEAFCUTTER ANTS

These busy ants are the gardeners of the rain forest.

Leafcutter ants live in a large group, called a colony. The colony builds a nest underground with a maze of tunnels.

The ants work together to feed the colony. Some of them travel through the forest to find leaves and flowers.

FACTS

KIND OF ANIMAL
insect

HOME
Central and South America

SIZE
can be as long as the word "home" above; queen ant can be longer

FOOD
fungus

SOUNDS
squeaks and drumming

BABIES
thousands of eggs a day

One leafcutter ant **COLONY** can have **MILLIONS** of **ANTS.**

Carrying the **LEAVES** on their **BACKS** helps hide the ants from **PREDATORS.**

The ant **COLONY** has a **QUEEN.** She is the only ant in the colony that **LAYS EGGS.**

Clip, snip. The ants slice off big pieces using their strong jaws. Then they haul the leaves on their backs to their nest. Back and forth they go, in a long, single line.

They deliver the leaves to smaller leafcutter ants. The smaller ants crunch the leaves until they are soft and mushy. Then they take the mush to a special part of their nest. This is where they grow their food, which is a kind of fungus.

The mashed–up leaves help the fungus grow. Later, all the ants will feed on the fungus.

JAWS

Where have you seen ants?

41

GIANT ANTEATER

The giant anteater **DOESN'T HAVE** any **TEETH.** It swallows its food **WHOLE.**

This animal is named for what it loves to eat—ants!

FACTS

KIND OF ANIMAL
mammal

HOME
Central and South America

SIZE
about the size of a large dog

FOOD
ants and termites

SOUNDS
grunts and squeals

BABIES
one at a time

Sniff, sniff. With its long, slender snout, the giant anteater can sniff out food that is far away.

When the anteater finds a mound of ants or termites, it uses its long, sharp claws to dig an opening. Then its sticky tongue flicks in and out as it slurps its food. How many ants and termites does this giant need to eat every day? 35,000!

The **GIANT** anteater's **TONGUE** can reach up to two feet (0.6 m) beyond its **MOUTH.**

The giant anteater walks on all fours. But if it is afraid, it stands up on its back legs and lashes out with its front claws.

This spider is about as **BIG** as a **DINNER PLATE.**

FACTS

KIND OF ANIMAL
arachnid

HOME
northern South America

FOOD
small mammals, frogs, lizards, and insects

SOUNDS
hisses

BABIES
200 eggs at a time

SIZE
This shows how big the spider is.

FIVE-YEAR-OLD

GOLIATH BIRD-EATING SPIDER

Meet the world's heaviest spider.

The goliath bird-eating spider lives in holes, or burrows, on the rain forest floor. It is a kind of tarantula. Tarantulas are large, hairy spiders. Like all spiders, they have eight legs.

Even though it has eight eyes, this spider doesn't see very well. But with the sensitive hairs on its legs, it feels vibrations when an animal is near. In a flash, the goliath bird-eating spider races out of hiding and grabs its prey.

This spider got its **NAME** because it is **BIG** enough to **EAT** a small **BIRD.** But it usually eats rats, mice, and insects.

Meet a few more spiders that live in **RAIN FORESTS.**

WANDERING SPIDER (SOUTH AMERICA)

WOLF SPIDER (SOUTH AMERICA)

PINKTOE TARANTULA (SOUTH AMERICA)

FISHING SPIDER (SOUTH AMERICA)

JUMPING SPIDER (ASIA)

CRAB SPIDER (SOUTH AMERICA)

Where have you seen spiderwebs?

CHAPTER 3
LIFE IN THE SHADOWY UNDERSTORY

The small trees and twisting vines of the understory are home to many animals. In this chapter, you will meet a few of them.

BEE HUMMINGBIRD

The bee hummingbird is the smallest bird in the world.

They may be tiny, but bee hummingbirds are mighty. When they are flying, their wings beat 80 times a second. That's so fast that humans can't even see the wings move.

Like all hummingbirds, this one can fly backward, sideways, and upside down. Its wings help it stay in place while it sips sweet nectar from flowers.

A bee hummingbird can visit as many as 1,500 flowers in one day!

FACTS

KIND OF ANIMAL
bird

HOME
Cuba

FOOD
flower nectar and insects

SOUNDS
high-pitched chirp

BABIES
two eggs at a time

SIZE
This shows how big this bird is.

FIVE-YEAR-OLD'S HAND

Bee hummingbirds need to **EAT** half their **WEIGHT** in food every **DAY.**

They get their **NAME** because they are about the **SIZE** of **BEES.**

What is something sweet that you like to drink?

This beetle has **SHARP CLAWS** on each of its **SIX LEGS.** The claws help it climb on trees.

What are some other animals with stripes?

GOLIATH BEETLE

This insect is part of the cleanup crew of the rain forest.

The goliath beetle has a special job. It eats rotted plants and the poop of other animals. That helps keep the forest clean.

HORNS

FACTS

KIND OF ANIMAL
insect

HOME
Africa

SIZE
about as long as an adult human's hand

FOOD
fruit, tree sap, and animal poop

SOUNDS
thrumming, like a helicopter

BABIES
about 40 to 60 eggs at a time

Goliath beetles are the heaviest beetles on the planet. They have white stripes on their upper backs. Males have Y-shaped horns they use to fight with other male goliaths.

Like most beetles, a goliath has two pairs of wings. The hard top pair protects its body. The pair folded underneath is used for flying.

KINKAJOU

This animal's nickname is the honey bear!

FACTS

KIND OF ANIMAL
mammal

HOME
Central and northern
South America

SIZE
about the size of a
house cat

FOOD
fruit, honey, and
insects

SOUNDS
squeaks, squeals, and
barks

BABIES
one or two at a time

SAY MY NAME:
KIN-
kuh-joo

During the day, the kinkajou rests in trees of
the understory and canopy. When night comes,
it wakes up and searches the rain forest for food.

It uses its long, fluffy **TAIL** as a **BLANKET** while it **SLEEPS.**

When it's **HAPPY,** the kinkajou makes a **SOUND** like a noisy kiss. **MWAH!**

The kinkajou uses its long tongue to slurp honey out of beehives. It also likes to nibble on sweet fruit that it can hold in its front paws.

The kinkajou's long tail helps it grab branches. It can also hang by its tail. Its rear feet can twist around to help it run backward up a tree!

Can you think of another animal that can hang by its tail?

PARSON'S CHAMELEON

This colorful lizard looks like a small dinosaur.

The Parson's chameleon's body is tall and thin. Its narrow shape helps the animal balance on slender branches. Its long tail curls around a branch to help it hold on.

MITTEN-SHAPED FEET help this chameleon **GRAB** on to branches.

FACTS

KIND OF ANIMAL
reptile

HOME
the island of Madagascar, off the coast of Africa

SIZE
about the size of a small house cat

FOOD
insects

SOUNDS
no known sound

BABIES
20 to 25 eggs at a time

Chameleons change their skin color to **WARM** or **COOL** their bodies. It takes about **20 SECONDS** for a chameleon's skin to **CHANGE** color.

Like other chameleons, the Parson's chameleon can change the color and pattern of its skin. It can be green or brown or even blue.

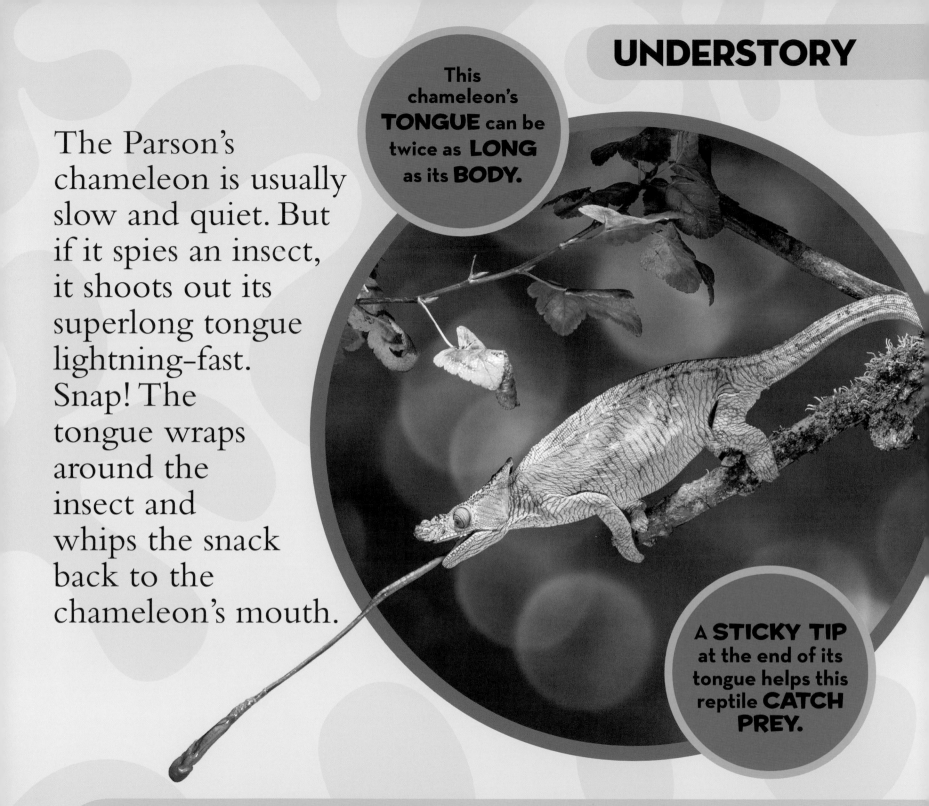

This chameleon's **TONGUE** can be twice as **LONG** as its **BODY**.

A **STICKY TIP** at the end of its tongue helps this reptile **CATCH PREY.**

The Parson's chameleon is usually slow and quiet. But if it spies an insect, it shoots out its superlong tongue lightning-fast. Snap! The tongue wraps around the insect and whips the snack back to the chameleon's mouth.

Can you think of another animal in this book that has a really long tongue? Hint: It eats ants.

ORCHID MANTIS

The orchid mantis is tricky.

This insect does a great job of looking like a flower. Its back legs fan out like petals.

The orchid mantis waits among the leaves and blossoms. When a moth or fly comes close, the orchid mantis snatches the insect with its long, spiny front legs.

An orchid mantis can attract more insects than flowers do! It can even fool a predator into thinking it's a flower and leaving it alone.

The orchid mantis can **TURN ITS HEAD AROUND** and look behind itself.

FACTS

KIND OF ANIMAL
insect

HOME
Southeast Asia

SIZE
males are about the size of a teaspoon; females are larger

FOOD
moths, crickets, and other insects

SOUNDS
hisses

BABIES
50 to 100 eggs at a time

The orchid mantis is a type of **PRAYING MANTIS.** Praying mantises can be found in **MANY PARTS** of the world. But orchid mantises live **ONLY** in **RAIN FORESTS.**

Can you imitate, or pretend to be, an animal?

ROUGH SCALES help protect the eyelash viper's body from **SPIKY** tree **BRANCHES.**

FACTS

KIND OF ANIMAL
reptile

HOME
Central and northern South America

SIZE
nearly as long as a guitar

FOOD
frogs, lizards, small birds, and mice

SOUNDS
soft slurping

BABIES
six to 20 live babies at a time

EYELASH VIPER
This beautiful snake has a deadly bite.

The eyelash viper can be yellow, green, brown, or even light blue. Its head is shaped like a triangle. This snake looks like it has eyelashes. But those are actually pointy scales.

The eyelash viper **BITES ITS PREY** with venom-filled **FANGS** to kill it.

The viper loops itself around trees, vines, flowers, and fruits in the understory. Its color helps it blend in with a plant or flower while it waits for its prey to come close. Hummingbirds are a favorite meal.

Feel your eyelashes—are they soft or scaly?

JAGUAR

Jaguars are big spotted cats.

The jaguar can be hard to see. Its spots help it blend in with the dappled light and shade of the understory. That helps the jaguar hide from animals it wants to eat.

During the day, this big cat snoozes in the trees. As the sun goes down, it walks out of its shadowy hiding place. It creeps along quietly. When it spots its prey, it pounces. *Whomp!*

FACTS

KIND OF ANIMAL
mammal

HOME
Central and South America

SIZE
can be as long as a bed

FOOD
sloths, deer, monkeys, birds, turtles, and frogs

SOUNDS
barklike roar

BABIES
one to four at a time

Jaguars are good **SWIMMERS.** They **HUNT** for **FISH** and **TURTLES** in the water.

Can you name some other things with spots?

A **MOTHER** jaguar **GUARDS** her **CUBS** from other animals.

Jaguar cubs stay with their mother until they are about two years old. She shows them everything they need to know to live on their own, including how to hunt.

Most jaguars are **ORANGE** or **TAN** with **BLACK SPOTS**, but some have such **DARK FUR** that it's hard to see their spots.

Jaguars are not the only wild cats that live in rain forests. Here are three more.

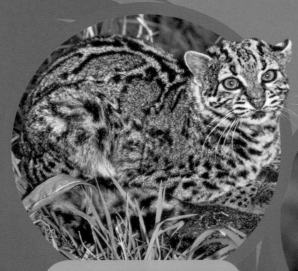

MARBLED CAT,
Asia

OCELOT,
South America

JAGUARONDI,
South America

67

KIND OF ANIMAL
mammal

HOME
the Philippines, in
Southeast Asia

SIZE
wingspan about as
long as a bathtub

FOOD
figs and other fruits

SOUNDS
squeaks and screeches

BABIES
one at a time

Bats are
the **ONLY**
MAMMALS
that can **FLY.**

GOLDEN-CROWNED FLYING FOX

The flying fox is actually a bat.

The flying fox **WRAPS ITS WINGS** around itself and rests **UPSIDE DOWN** from a branch.

This bat gets its name because its face reminds people of a fox's face. It has a ring of golden fur around its neck.

During the day, the flying fox sleeps in trees or caves. At night, it flies off to find fruit to eat. Sometimes the flying fox travels more than 20 miles (32 km) in search of its favorite food—figs.

What is your favorite fruit?

Young chicks have **CLAWS** on the end of their **WINGS** to help them **CLIMB** on tree branches.

Can you think of another animal that makes stinky smells?

HOATZIN

This bird is sometimes called the stink bird.

These big birds eat leaves. A hoatzin takes a long time to digest its food, so the leaves sit in its digestive system for a while. After a few days, these leaves start to stink—and so does the bird when it burps!

Hoatzins build their nests in branches over water. When a hungry monkey or snake comes near the nest, the chicks jump into the water below. When the danger has gone, the chicks swim to shore. Then they climb back up the tree into the nest.

FACTS

KIND OF ANIMAL
bird

HOME
northern South America

SIZE
an average-size cat

FOOD
leaves

SOUNDS
grunts, squawks, and hisses

BABIES
two or three eggs at a time

SAY MY NAME:
wat-SEEN

GREEN IGUANA

This reptile has spiky scales along its back.

FACTS

KIND OF ANIMAL
reptile

HOME
Central and South America

SIZE
longer than an average-size man

FOOD
leaves, flowers, and fruit

SOUNDS
purring, squeaking

BABIES
up to 70 eggs at a time

Green iguanas are large lizards. Even though they are called green iguanas, they can change color from brown to green and sometimes to turquoise.

The green iguana knows if something is moving above it without looking up. That's because it has a third eye on top of its head. This eye is not the same as the iguana's other eyes. It helps the lizard see moving shadows, so it knows if a predator is about to swoop in and grab it.

Iguanas lay leathery **EGGS** in burrows in the ground. The **BABIES** use a **SPECIAL TOOTH** to crack the egg from the inside.

SPIKES

BIRDS and snakes PREY on IGUANAS.

If a **GREEN** iguana is caught by the **TAIL,** it can release its tail and leave it behind. It will **GROW** another.

73

CHAPTER 4
LIFE IN THE LEAFY GREEN CANOPY

Many animals climb, crawl, and fly high in this layer of the rain forest. In this chapter you will meet birds, monkeys, frogs, and a few animals you may not know.

KIND OF ANIMAL
bird

HOME
Central and South America

SIZE
about as long as a human baby

FOOD
berries, other fruits, and eggs

SOUNDS
loud barks, croaks, and toots

BABIES
one to five eggs at a time

The **TOCO TOUCAN** uses its **SHARP BILL** to slice through banana peels. The edges of its bill are **NOTCHED**, like a saw.

How many colors do you see on this toucan?

TOCO TOUCAN

This bird has a brightly colored bill.

The toco toucan's big bill looks heavy, but it's not. The inside of it contains a lot of air, which makes it light. The toucan uses its long bill to pluck berries or fruit at the tip of a branch.

Sometimes these birds **PLAY GAMES** like catch—with **FRUIT!**

The toucan's feet have two toes facing forward and two facing backward. This helps it balance on branches when it looks for food.

77

HOWLER MONKEY

Meet the loudest animal in the rain forest.

A **GROUP** of monkeys is called a **TROOP.**

As soon as they wake up, howler monkeys roar. They roar again before they go to sleep at night. These noisy animals want others to know where they are— and to stay away!

Howler monkeys are **ARBOREAL.** That means they **LIVE** in **TREES.**

A howler monkey's cry sounds something like a lion's roar, or a very long, loud burp. It can be heard two to three miles (3.2 to 4.8 km) away!

FACTS

KIND OF ANIMAL
mammal

HOME
Central and South America

SIZE
not including its tail, about the size of a two-year-old human

FOOD
leaves, fruit, nuts, and flowers

SOUNDS
earsplitting roar

BABIES
one at a time

What other loud animals can you name?

Many different kinds of **MONKEYS** make their homes in the **RAIN FOREST CANOPY** or **UNDERSTORY**. Here are a few of them.

NIGHT MONKEY (SOUTH AMERICA)

COLOBUS MONKEY (AFRICA)

SPIDER MONKEY
(CENTRAL AND SOUTH AMERICA)

SQUIRREL MONKEY
(CENTRAL AND SOUTH AMERICA)

EMPEROR TAMARIN (SOUTH AMERICA)

FACTS

KIND OF ANIMAL
mammal

HOME
Australia, Indonesia, and New Guinea

SIZE
not including the tail, about the size of a man's hand

FOOD
nectar, insects, and tree sap

SOUNDS
barking, chattering, and chirping

BABIES
one or two at a time

Sugar gliders are **MARSUPIALS.** Like most marsupials, they carry their **BABIES** in a **POUCH.**

SUGAR GLIDER

This animal is named for its love of sweet foods.

Sugar gliders are **NOCTURNAL**. That means they are **ACTIVE** at **NIGHT**.

The sugar glider has a thin, furry flap of skin that runs down the sides of its body from its front to back feet. When the animal spreads its legs wide, the flaps stretch out, like wings.

During the day, sugar gliders rest in nests in trees. At night, they sail through the air from tree to tree, looking for sweet nectar and tree sap to eat.

RAGGIANA BIRD OF PARADISE

This bird really puts on a show!

The male Raggiana bird of paradise has a pale yellow head. His beak is surrounded by green feathers. Most of this beautiful bird's feathers are fiery orange.

Rrawk! Crrrreetcoo! That's the male singing to attract a female bird. Then the male puffs out his chest. He claps his wings together. Next, he fluffs up his tail. Finally, he tap-dances up and down the tree branch.

SAY MY NAME: RAH-gee-ah-nah

FACTS

KIND OF ANIMAL
bird

HOME
Papua New Guinea

SIZE
about the size of a man's foot

FOOD
berries, other fruits, and lizards

SOUNDS
squawks and trills

BABIES
one to two eggs at a time

84

Bird of paradise **CHICKS** are **BORN** with no **FEATHERS.**

Some types of birds of paradise **HANG UPSIDE DOWN** to **ATTRACT FEMALES.**

Can you sing and dance at the same time?

BLACK-AND-WHITE RUFFED LEMUR

The ruff of white fur under its chin gives this lemur its name.

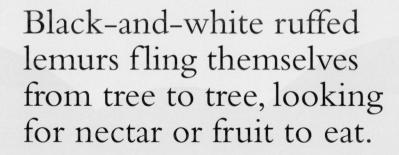

Black-and-white ruffed lemurs fling themselves from tree to tree, looking for nectar or fruit to eat.

Ruffed lemurs build nests high in the trees. A mother ruffed lemur gives birth to her babies there. If she needs to leave the nest to find food, the father lemur helps guard the babies.

LEMURS are related to MONKEYS.

There are many different kinds of **LEMURS.** They are found in the **WILD** only on Madagascar, a large island off the coast of **AFRICA.**

After a week or two, the mother lemur moves her babies out of the nest and onto the tree branches. She carries them gently in her mouth.

FACTS

KIND OF ANIMAL
mammal

HOME
Madagascar, Africa

SIZE
about the size of a large house cat

FOOD
fruit, seeds, and leaves

SOUNDS
howls, shrieks, and roars

BABIES
two or three at a time

What are some other black-and-white animals?

THREE-TOED SLOTH

This slow-moving animal sleeps most of the day away.

A sloth spends almost all its **LIFE** in the **TREES.** It comes down to the ground only about **ONCE A WEEK,** to poop.

The three-toed sloth spends a lot of time hanging on to tree branches. It often hangs upside down.

FACTS

KIND OF ANIMAL
mammal

HOME
Central and South America

SIZE
about as big as a medium-size dog

FOOD
leaves, shoots, and fruits

SOUNDS
call of *AHH-EEE*

BABIES
one at a time

Can you think of another animal that moves very slowly?

Sloths are good **SWIMMERS.** If they accidentally **TUMBLE** out of a tree into water, they can **SWIM** to shore and climb another tree.

Sloths move super slowly through trees, munching on juicy leaves. Sometimes they don't move at all, so it's hard to tell if they are awake or asleep!

Tiny plantlike organisms called green algae grow on the three-toed sloth's fur. The algae give the fur a greenish color. This helps the sloth blend into the trees and hide from animals that might want to eat it.

JAGUARS and **HARPY EAGLES HUNT** sloths.

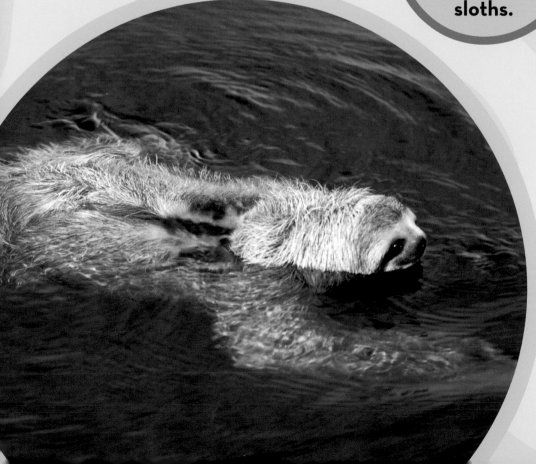

Sloths have long, curved claws on each of their toes. These claws are perfect for hanging on to trees. But they make walking impossible. On the forest floor, the three-toed sloth drags itself along on its belly.

91

FACTS

KIND OF ANIMAL
mammal

HOME
Indonesia and the Philippines, in Southeast Asia

SIZE
about as big as a man's hand

FOOD
insects, spiders, and lizards

SOUNDS
chirps, trills, and loud calls

BABIES
one at a time

Its long **TAIL** helps the tarsier **BALANCE** and **STEER** as it jumps among the **TREES**.

How far around can you turn your head?

TARSIER

This wee animal has enormous eyes.

SAY MY NAME: TAR-see-er

The tarsier hunts at night. Its big eyes help it see in the dark. The tarsier can turn its head so far around that it can almost see behind itself.

When this animal spies an insect or other prey, it pounces on it and grabs it with both hands.

This animal can **WIGGLE** each **EAR** separately.

The tarsier uses its long, strong back legs to jump and leap about in the trees. Its fingers and toes have round pads on the ends that help it hold on tightly to tree trunks.

93

ORANGUTAN

Orangutans spend most of their time in the trees.

Orangutans have shaggy fur and long arms. They travel through the rain forest by scampering up tree trunks and swinging from branch to branch with their strong arms.

Before dark, orangutans bend down branches to make comfy nests in the trees to sleep in. They hardly ever use the same nest twice.

FACTS

KIND OF ANIMAL
mammal

HOME
Indonesia and Malaysia, in Southeast Asia

SIZE
can be as small as a ten-year-old human or as big as an average-size man

FOOD
fruits, leaves, and insects

SOUNDS
rumbles, howls, and booms

BABIES
one every five to eight years

The word "orangutan" means "**PERSON OF THE FOREST**" in the **MALAY** language.

Because of their **COLOR,** orangutans are sometimes called **RED APES.**

When it **RAINS**, orangutans sometimes hold **LARGE LEAVES** over their heads—just as people use **UMBRELLAS**.

Sometimes orangutans **MAKE NESTS** to **NAP** in during the **DAY**.

When it is first born, a baby orangutan clings tightly to its mother's tummy. Later, it will ride piggyback.

Even when they can climb by themselves, young orangutans stay with their mothers. They don't live on their own until they are six or seven years old.

What animals live in trees near your home?

EMERALD TREE BOA

This snake is named after a green gemstone called an emerald.

The emerald tree boa slithers through the canopy, coiling itself around high tree branches. When it rains, water pools in its coils. The snake uses this water to drink.

Like the green anaconda on page 22, the emerald tree boa is a constrictor. When it spots a lizard or small mammal, it lunges. Then it wraps itself around the animal and squeezes to kill it before eating it.

FACTS

KIND OF ANIMAL
reptile

HOME
South America

SIZE
longer than an average-size man

FOOD
lizards, squirrels, and monkeys

SOUNDS
none that scientists know of

BABIES
up to 20 live babies at a time

BOA constrictors are **GOOD** at feeling **MOVEMENTS** of other animals.

Most emerald tree boas are born **BRICK RED.** Some are born yellow or orange. As they grow, they all turn **BRIGHT GREEN.**

Tree kangaroos are **NOCTURNAL.** They search for **FOOD** at **NIGHT** and sleep during the day.

FACTS

KIND OF ANIMAL
mammal

HOME
New Guinea, Indonesia, and Australia

SIZE
about the size of a medium-size dog

FOOD
leaves and fruit

SOUNDS
clicks and coughs

BABIES
one a year

The tree kangaroo **CLIMBS** down trees **TAIL** first.

TREE KANGAROO

The tree kangaroo has a fluffy coat.

Most kangaroos hop around on the ground. But a few live in trees. They are called tree kangaroos. They have stronger front paws than ground kangaroos. These paws help them climb in the trees.

Like all kangaroos, tree kangaroos are marsupials. The mothers carry their babies in their built-in pouch.

A **BABY** kangaroo is called a **JOEY.**

Can you find another marsupial in this book? Hint: Look on page 82.

This big bird **PICKS UP** its **FOOD** with its long, curved beak.

FACTS

KIND OF ANIMAL
bird

HOME
Southeast Asia

SIZE
about as long as a
three-year-old child

FOOD
mostly fruit, also insects,
lizards, and frogs.

SOUNDS
hok, hok call

BABIES
one or two eggs at a time

RHINOCEROS HORNBILL

This bird is named for the huge, hornlike growth on the top of its beak.

The rhinoceros hornbill swoops around in the canopy looking for fruit to eat.

When a female hornbill is ready to lay eggs, she looks for a hole in a tree trunk. She lays one or two eggs inside. Then she and the father bird seal the trunk with mud while she stays inside. They leave a small slit for food.

When the chicks are a few months old, the mother bird pecks her way out of the nest. She helps the father find food for the baby birds.

When a hornbill **FLIES**, its huge wings make a **LOUD** whooshing sound.

FACTS

KIND OF ANIMAL
amphibian

HOME
Mexico and Central America

SIZE
about as long as a man's pointer finger

FOOD
insects

SOUNDS
barking and croaking

BABIES
hundreds of eggs at a time

What color are your eyes?

RED-EYED TREE FROG

This animal has orange feet and blue markings on its legs.

At night, red-eyed tree frogs climb and leap through the treetops. They hunt for insects to eat. They catch their meal with their long, sticky tongues.

During the day, this frog sleeps on green leaves. It tucks its feet under its body, so its bright colors are hidden. That helps the frog blend in with the leaf and hide from hungry birds and snakes.

The red-eyed tree frog has **PADS** on its **TOES** that stick like **SUCTION CUPS** to leaves and branches.

CHAPTER 5
FLYING HIGH IN THE EMERGENT LAYER

In this chapter, you will meet some of the creatures that live in the tip-top of the rain forest.

FACTS

KIND OF ANIMAL
bird

HOME
Central and South America

FOOD
lizards, birds, monkeys, sloths, and other mammals

SOUNDS
wails, croaks, and whistles

BABIES
one or two eggs

SIZE
This shows how big a harpy eagle is.

FIVE-YEAR-OLD

This bird's **TALONS,** or claws, are larger than a grizzly bear's **CLAWS.**

HARPY EAGLE

This huge bird has excellent eyesight.

From its perch in the tallest trees of the rain forest, a harpy eagle keeps watch for prey. When it spies an iguana, monkey, or sloth, the bird swoops down and snatches it with its big, sharp claws.

Male and female harpy eagles usually stay together for life. They build a giant nest—big enough for two grown men!

Can you think of another kind of eagle? Hint: It is a symbol of the United States.

QUEEN ALEXANDRA'S BIRDWING BUTTERFLY

Meet the largest butterfly in the world.

MALE

Female Queen Alexandra's birdwing butterflies are **LARGER** than the males. A female's wingspan can be wider than the cover **OF THIS BOOK!**

FEMALE

These beautiful butterflies flit and flutter in the highest treetops of the rain forest.

The males and females look different from each other. A male's wings are shimmery blue-green on top, and blue and yellow on the bottom. A female has mostly brown wings.

MALE

FACTS

KIND OF ANIMAL
insect

HOME
Papua New Guinea

FOOD
leaves for caterpillars;
flower nectar for adult
butterflies

SOUNDS
only wing-flapping noise

BABIES
about 15 to 20 eggs at a
time

SIZE
This shows how big a
female birdwing is.

FIVE-YEAR-OLD

How big are the butterflies you have seen?

Rain forests around the **WORLD** are **HOME** to thousands of different kinds of **BUTTERFLIES.** Here are just a few.

BLUE MORPHO (CENTRAL AND SOUTH AMERICA)

BLUE DOCTOR (SOUTH AMERICA)

POSTMAN (CENTRAL AND SOUTH AMERICA)

CLEARWING SWALLOWTAIL (AUSTRALIA)

RED DAGGERWING
(CENTRAL AND SOUTH AMERICA)

BLUE-AND-YELLOW MACAW

These big birds make a lot of noise.

Blue-and-yellow macaws are chatty birds. They screech and squawk to talk to each other.

During the day, blue-and-yellow macaws fly from tree to tree, searching for fruit and nuts to eat. They use their strong beaks to crack open hard nuts.

FACTS

KIND OF ANIMAL
bird

HOME
Central and South America

SIZE
longer than a two-year-old human

FOOD
seeds, nuts, and fruit

SOUNDS
squawks and screeches

BABIES
two or three eggs

A macaw can **PICK UP** food with its claws and bring it to its **MOUTH.**

Macaws can **COPY SOUNDS** of other animals.

MACAWS are a kind of **PARROT.** Here are some other parrots that live in the **CANOPY** and **EMERGENT LAYERS** of the **RAIN FOREST.**

SCARLET MACAWS (CENTRAL AND SOUTH AMERICA)

RAINBOW LORIKEET (AUSTRALIA)

GREAT GREEN MACAW
(CENTRAL AND SOUTH AMERICA)

AFRICAN GRAY PARROT (AFRICA)

HYACINTH MACAW (SOUTH AMERICA)

10 COOL THINGS TO REMEMBER ABOUT RAIN FORESTS!

1
Most **RAIN FORESTS** get at least **100 INCHES** (254 cm) of rain a year.

2
Most of Earth's rain forests are found in the **TROPICS,** the parts of the planet **CLOSE TO THE EQUATOR,** where it stays **WARM** all year.

3
A rain forest has **FOUR** different **LAYERS:** forest floor, understory, canopy, and emergent layer.

4
About half of all types of **PLANTS** and **ANIMALS** on Earth **LIVE** in rain forests.

5
The **WORLD'S SMALLEST BIRD** lives in the rain forest.

7
BANANAS, ORANGES, PINEAPPLES, and many other fruits we eat were first discovered **GROWING** in tropical rain forests.

8
CHOCOLATE is made from the **BEANS** of the **CACAO TREE,** which was first found growing in rain forests in Central America and South America.

6
The world's biggest **BUTTERFLY** makes its **HOME** in the **RAIN FOREST.**

9
Not all rain forests are tropical. Some, called **TEMPERATE** rain forests, grow in **COOLER PARTS** of the world. The **TREES** and **ANIMALS** found there are **DIFFERENT** from those in tropical rain forests.

10
The world's rain forests are very **SPECIAL PLACES.** They are home to countless animals and plants. That is why it is so important to **PROTECT** rain forests and keep them healthy. You can **HELP** by sharing what you've learned about rain forests and the plants and animals that live there.

PARENT TIPS

Extend your child's experience beyond the pages of this book. Visit a forest or find a park nearby and go for a walk. Point out the tallest trees. Then look at the low-growing plants and trees. Talk about how different the leaves are. Look for birds and insects and other animals. If you find any that can be safely examined, explore how their unique bodies are adapted for where they live. Here are some other activities you can do with National Geographic's *Little Kids First Big Book of the Rain Forest*.

IT'S A ZOO (OBSERVATION)

Many zoos have rain forest exhibits. If you live near one of these exhibits or are traveling to a place that has one, walk through it with your child. Ask her to describe how the moisture in the air feels on her skin. Point out the forest floor, and try to find animals and insects there. If the understory and canopy levels are featured in the exhibit, ask your child what animals she can spot in them.

HOW DO YOU SIZE UP? (MATH)

Spread out a long roll of paper, taller than your child. Ask your child to lie down on top of the paper, then trace the outline of his body on it. Measure the length of the outline with a yardstick or tape measure, then mark your child's height on the paper. Select six or seven animals from this book. Using the yardstick, mark on the drawing how tall the animals are in relation to your child.

HOWL LIKE A HOWLER MONKEY (SOUNDS)

Roar! Krawk! Hiss! Burrrrp! The animals of the rain forest can make a lot of noise. Let your child pick a few animals. Read how their sounds are described. Try to find a recording on the Internet of the animal's sounds. Then ask your child to imitate the sound the animal makes. You might want to join in—it can be a lot of fun!

CREATE A RAIN FOREST COLLAGE (ARTS AND CRAFTS)

Help your child make a colorful rain forest collage. Find photos from magazines or cut up construction paper to create trees and leaves. Use a glue stick to attach them to poster board. Then add pictures or drawings of animals such as monkeys, birds, and snakes. Sprinkle glitter over the collage to represent the rain.

SLITHER LIKE A SNAKE (EXERCISE)

The animals in this book move in a lot of different ways. Encourage your child to demonstrate how some of them move. She can slither on her belly like a snake, flutter her arms like a butterfly's wings, or hop like a frog. She can pretend to shoot out her tongue like a chameleon or inch along very, very slowly, like a sloth.

OVER THE RAINBOW (COLORS)

Many animals that live in rain forests are brightly colored. Find a large photo of a rainbow. Identify the seven colors of the rainbow: red, orange, yellow, green, blue, indigo, and violet. Then, look through the pictures in this book with your child. Help him find the animals that are primarily one of each of the colors of the rainbow.

ANIMAL MAP

Use this world map to see on which continents the animals featured in this book can be found in the wild.

ARCTIC

PACIFIC OCEAN

NORTH AMERICA

ATLANTIC OCEAN

SOUTH AMERICA

NORTH AMERICA

Bee Hummingbird
Blue-and-Yellow Macaw
Capybara
Eyelash Viper
Giant Anteater
Green Iguana
Harpy Eagle
Howler Monkey
Jaguar
Kinkajou
Leafcutter Ant
Red-Eyed Tree Frog
Three-Toed Sloth

SOUTH AMERICA

Amazon River Dolphin
Blue Poison Dart Frog
Blue-and-Yellow Macaw
Capybara
Emerald Tree Boa
Eyelash Viper
Giant Anteater
Goliath Bird-Eating Spider
Green Anaconda
Green Iguana
Harpy Eagle
Hoatzin
Howler Monkey
Jaguar
Kinkajou
Leafcutter Ant
Lowland Tapir
Three-Toed Sloth
Toco Toucan

Where tropical rain forests are found

OCEAN

MAP

EUROPE

ASIA

ASIA
Golden-Crowned Flying Fox
Orangutan
Orchid Mantis
Rhinoceros Hornbill
Tarsier

AFRICA

PACIFIC
OCEAN

EQUATOR

INDIAN
OCEAN

OCEANIA

AUSTRALIA

AFRICA
Black-and-White Ruffed Lemur
Goliath Beetle
Lowland Streaked Tenrec
Mandrill
Parson's Chameleon

AUSTRALIA
AND OCEANIA
Queen Alexandra's Birdwing Butterfly
Raggiana Bird of Paradise
Southern Cassowary
Sugar Glider
Tree Kangaroo

ANTARCTICA

GLOSSARY

AMPHIBIANS: a group of cold-blooded animals with backbones (vertebrate); in some species, larval young live in water and breathe through gills; includes frogs, toads, and salamanders

ARACHNIDS: a group of animals with no backbone (invertebrate), two body segments, and two to four pairs of legs; includes spiders, scorpions, mites, and ticks

ARBOREAL: living in trees

BIRDS: a group of warm-blooded, vertebrate animals that have feathers, wings, and lay eggs; most can fly

BROMELIAD: a flowering plant that grows on trees and in rain forests

DIGESTIVE SYSTEM: a group of body parts, including the stomach, that works to turn food into energy

EQUATOR: an imaginary line around the Earth that divides the planet into northern and southern hemispheres, or halves

FUNGUS: a living thing that is not a plant, animal, or bacteria; includes mold, mildew, yeast, and mushrooms; the food that leafcutter ants make is a fungus

INSECTS: any of a group of small, invertebrate animals with three body segments, one pair of antennae, and three pairs of legs; often have wings

INVERTEBRATE: animals without spinal columns, or backbones

JUNGLE: a tropical forest

LIANA: a thick, woody vine that grows in rain forests

MAMMALS: a group of vertebrate animals, including humans, that are warm-blooded, breathe air, have hair, and nurse their young

MARSUPIALS: an order of mammals whose females generally carry their young in pouches on their abdomen

NOCTURNAL: active at night

PREDATOR: an animal that eats other animals (prey)

PREY: an animal that a predator hunts for food

REPTILES: a group of vertebrate animals that are cold-blooded, usually slither (such as snakes) or walk on short legs (such as turtles and lizards); generally covered with scales or bony plates

TROPICAL: relating to a warm region or climate that is frost-free

VERTEBRATES: animals that have a spinal column, or backbone

ADDITIONAL RESOURCES

BOOKS

Delano, Marfe Ferguson. *Explore My World: Rain Forests*. National Geographic, 2017.

Esbaum, Jill. *Angry Birds: Playground Rain Forest*. National Geographic, 2014.

Hughes, Catherine D. *Little Kids First Big Book of Animals*. National Geographic, 2011.

Lawler, Janet. *Rain Forest Colors*. National Geographic, 2014.

Mitchell, Susan K. *The Rainforest Grew All Around*. Sylvan Dell, 2007.

Neuman, Susan B. *Swing, Sloth! Explore the Rain Forest*. National Geographic, 2014.

Stewart, Melissa. *No Monkeys, No Chocolate*. Charlesbridge, 2013.

WEBSITES

kids.mongabay.com

natgeokids.com/explore/nature/habitats/rain-forest

INDEX

**TO MY NIECES, ALEXANDRA AND EMILY,
WHO ARE EVEN MORE BEAUTIFUL THAN THE RAIN FOREST —MRD**

Since 1888, the National Geographic Society has funded more than 12,000 research, exploration, and preservation projects around the world. The Society receives funds from National Geographic Partners, LLC, funded in part by your purchase. A portion of the proceeds from this book supports this vital work. To learn more, visit natgeo.com/info.

NATIONAL GEOGRAPHIC and Yellow Border Design are trademarks of the National Geographic Society, used under license.

For more information, visit nationalgeographic.com, call 1-877-873-6846, or write to the following address:

National Geographic Partners
1145 17th Street N.W.
Washington, D.C. 20036-4688 U.S.A.

Visit us online at nationalgeographic.com/books

For librarians and teachers: ngchildrensbooks.org

More for kids from National Geographic: natgeokids.com

For rights or permissions inquiries, please contact National Geographic Books Subsidiary Rights: bookrights@natgeo.com

Designed by Nicole Lazarus

Hardcover ISBN: 978-1-4263-3171-8
Reinforced library binding ISBN: 978-1-4263-3172-5

The publisher gratefully acknowledges conservation ecologist Dr. Thomas Lovejoy of George Mason University, Department of Environmental Science and Policy, for his expert review of this book and researcher Michelle Harris for her invaluable help with this project.

Printed in China
22/PPS/3